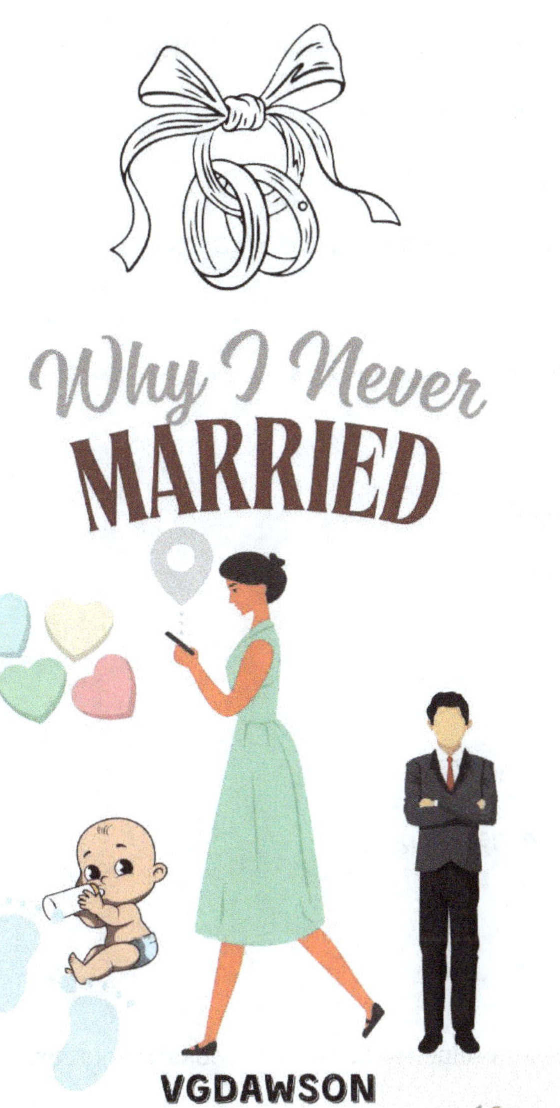

Why I Never MARRIED

VGDAWSON

SECOND SEASON PRESS

Books on Friendship, Relationships, and Personal Growth

Books on Personal Growth and Life Reflection

I Need to Think About My Life Choices

Unlocking Your Best Self

Guide to Self-Improvement in Seven Days

Books on Relationships and Personal Boundaries

Friendship Year

My Best Friend

Friends for Life

Friendless

Books for Young Readers

Guide to Teenage Dating

Discover More

Visit the author online for additional books, resources, and inspiration:

www.what2buynext.com

Why I Never Married? Unwed-Unshaken: Living Life on My Own Terms

Copyright © 2026 by VaNessa G. Dawson

Published by

Second Season Press

Birmingham, Alabama

www.what2buynext.com

ISBN: 978-1-972518-25-0

Cataloging information is available from the Library of Congress.

Library of Congress Control Number: 2026910514

First Edition: 2026

This book is a work of nonfiction. The information presented is based on the author's experiences and research and is intended for educational and informational purposes only. The author and publisher disclaim any liability for any injury, damage, or loss resulting from the use of the information contained herein. Readers are encouraged to seek professional guidance when appropriate.

All brand names and product names referenced in this book are trademarks or registered trademarks of their respective owners. Their use is for identification purposes only and does not imply endorsement.

Printed in the United States of America

To my beloved cousin, Lady Di,

This book is dedicated to you—

A woman of unmatched grace, quiet strength, and unwavering love.

For over forty years, you have selflessly dedicated your life to caring for our elders, nurturing the sick, and stepping in when others could not. You gave your youthful years not to a marriage or children of your own, but to the heartbeat of this family.

Through family conflicts, painful losses, moments of joy, and seasons of healing, you have been our anchor. The one who held the center when everything felt like it was falling apart. You weathered every storm with dignity, carried burdens without complaint, and led with a quiet courage that stitched this family back together time and time again.

Though life may have unfolded differently than you once imagined, you crafted a life of deep purpose, quiet power, and enduring love. Over the years, we have grown into a bond that reflects kindness, mutual respect, and profound honor.

I dedicate this book to you, Lady Di.

For the life you lived, the love you gave, and the legacy you continue to build—

You are truly amazing.

With love and deep admiration,
Vgdawson

Introduction

In a world where marriage is often seen as the ultimate milestone of a fulfilling life, there exists a quieter, lesser-told story of those who chose another path. This book, Why I Never Married? Unwed-Unshaken, Living Life on My Own Terms, is a celebration of lives lived with intention, strength, and purpose beyond the traditional bounds of matrimony. It's a journey into the lives of people who, for reasons uniquely their own, remained unmarried yet profoundly content and accomplished.

For centuries, society has impressed upon us the idea that to live fully, one must find a soulmate and walk through life side by side. But for some, the reality of a joyful, purpose-driven life unfolds differently. These are the stories of individuals who have built rich, meaningful lives on their own terms, who defy the notion that happiness can only be found in partnership. Their journeys are filled with laughter, heartbreak, success, and wisdom as they navigate careers, passions, friendships, and personal growth, each carving out a legacy that is uniquely theirs.

Through these pages, I'll introduce you to the idea that life without marriage is neither a lonely endeavor nor an unfulfilled one.

By listening to the voices of those who live fully without a ring on their finger, we'll uncover how independence can be just as powerful and affirming as companionship. Their experiences reveal that while marriage can be beautiful, it's not the only path to a life rich with love, purpose, and happiness.

Let this book serve as a reminder that fulfillment is not one-size-fits-all, and that living by our own choices, unshaken by expectations, is something worth celebrating.

Chapter 1:

Redefining Life Beyond Marriage

This chapter sets the foundation for understanding how individuals who choose not to marry redefine fulfillment and purpose in a world where partnership often takes center stage. It explores the social norms around marriage, how these have evolved, and what it takes to challenge them.

Each section examines how these individuals create their own standards of happiness, often developing deeper self-understanding, resilience, and a profound sense of independence along the way.

Challenging Social Norms

In many cultures, marriage is not only expected but often seen as a rite of passage into adulthood, success, and social legitimacy. Those who deviate from this norm frequently face misunderstandings or even stigmatization. For many of the individuals whose stories will be shared in this book, the choice not to marry has been both liberating and complex. This section discusses the courage and self-awareness it takes to resist societal pressure and build a life that aligns with one's values and beliefs.

To understand what it means to challenge social norms, we must first look at the historical context of marriage. Traditionally, marriage was not only about love or companionship but about survival, economic stability, and societal roles. However, as society has evolved, so too have our reasons for marrying, or choosing not to.

Today, people who remain unmarried are increasingly redefining what it means to be "successful" or "fulfilled," yet they often face lingering stereotypes. Common questions like "Why aren't you married?" or "Don't you want to settle down?" reflect deep-seated assumptions about what constitutes a meaningful life.

For some, choosing to remain single is a conscious decision to avoid relationships that don't align with their personal goals, beliefs, or sense of self. Many find that by not marrying, they are free to pursue passions, travel, and experience life on their terms. Others find fulfillment in careers or social contributions that would have been difficult within a traditional partnership.

This section also explores how friends, family, and society often view unmarried individuals through a lens of pity or incompleteness. Those who choose this path face questions that married people are rarely asked. But as we delve into the stories of these individuals, we'll see that redefining fulfillment requires a level of introspection and courage that leads them to unique and meaningful forms of happiness.

Embracing Self-Defined Happiness

If society suggests that happiness is best achieved within marriage, what happens when someone decides that marriage isn't part of their happiness equation? This section explores how those who remain unmarried develop a personal definition of happiness and how they pursue it in ways that are deeply satisfying and often unexpected.

Many people who choose a life outside of marriage are adept at cultivating self-love, confidence, and resilience. Their happiness comes from building lives filled with things they love—whether that's through career achievements, artistic pursuits, travel, or the development of deep friendships. By focusing on self-defined goals and dreams, they are often able to reach a level of fulfillment that some married individuals may struggle to find. This section will detail the personal narratives of individuals who found peace and joy by following paths that resonate with them, irrespective of societal expectations.

In crafting a life of self-defined happiness, they often experience moments of intense personal growth. By learning to meet their own emotional needs, they demonstrate that happiness does not require a partner but rather a commitment to one's own passions, growth, and dreams. For some, this means building close-knit communities of friends who serve as a support network instead of a traditional spouse.

For others, it's about achieving independence and learning the power of solitude. These stories illuminate how powerful and fulfilling life can be when we define happiness on our own terms.

One story highlights a woman who, in her 40s, left a high-stress corporate job to pursue her lifelong dream of traveling and photographing wildlife. Though friends and family were initially skeptical, assuming she'd regret choosing such an unconventional path alone, she ultimately found peace and joy in the freedom to pursue her dreams unencumbered. Her story underscores the idea that happiness, while often assumed to be found in companionship, can also come from a life filled with purpose and passion.

Another individual might share how dedicating his life to nonprofit work and education has brought him immense satisfaction. In his case, happiness doesn't come from romantic partnership but from the sense of legacy he's created through mentoring young people and investing in causes he believes in. His life is an example of how, by following a self-defined purpose, individuals can build lives that feel full and meaningful.

Summary:

In redefining life beyond marriage, individuals who remain single are often living as pioneers of a modern approach to fulfillment. They challenge norms, create their own versions of happiness, and show us all that life's joy is not confined to a single model. They remind us that marriage is one of many options for a fulfilling life, not a requirement.

Ultimately, Chapter 1 sets the stage for the chapters that follow, which delve into the rich, multifaceted lives these individuals lead. This chapter is an invitation to question assumptions, celebrate independence, and recognize that a single life can be just as rich, vibrant, and meaningful as any other.

Chapter 2:

Crafting a Purposeful Life

While marriage is often associated with stability and shared purpose, those who remain single have a unique opportunity to craft purpose in ways that may be even more expansive and varied. In this chapter, we explore how people who choose not to marry channel their energy and commitment into work, passion projects, community, and personal growth. Their lives illustrate how fulfilling and vibrant life can be when one's purpose is aligned with personal passions, ambitions, and values.

Career as a Calling

For many who remain unmarried, a career becomes a significant source of identity, satisfaction, and purpose. Unlike in a traditional marriage, where work-life balance can be challenging, a single person often has greater freedom to pursue their career in ways that bring them joy, growth, and a deep sense of accomplishment. This section explores how an individual's career can serve as both a calling and a primary focus in life, particularly for those who feel that their work brings value and meaning not only to themselves but also to society.

Consider the story of Maria, a doctor who always felt her calling was to help underserved communities.

Early in her career, she faced the question of whether to settle down and marry or to follow her passion for medicine, which would likely involve frequent relocations to regions in need. By choosing not to marry, Maria has been able to commit fully to her work without the added pressures of family obligations.

Her career has taken her across continents, allowing her to immerse herself in different cultures and positively impact countless lives. For Maria, the choice to remain single has provided a freedom that marriage could have limited, allowing her to invest fully in her calling and experience an incredibly purposeful life through her work.

This section also delves into how career-driven individuals often find profound satisfaction in professional achievements that align with their deepest values. Individuals like Maria don't view their work as merely a job; it's their mission, one that gives them a daily sense of purpose and self-worth.

Their dedication to a calling demonstrates that fulfillment doesn't have to stem from partnership; it can also come from the pursuit of meaningful work that leaves a legacy.

Another story focuses on Joshua, a teacher who decided early in life to dedicate himself to educating at-risk youth. For him, teaching is far more than a profession; it's a way to influence lives, to guide young people, and to give back to the community.

His work allows him to shape future generations, a role he sees as a form of legacy-building akin to raising a family. By channeling his energy and love into his students, Joshua finds a profound sense of purpose, one that feels every bit as fulfilling as traditional family life might be for someone else.

Passion Projects and Personal Fulfillment

Purpose doesn't only come from professional success; for many, it's also found in the passions, hobbies, and creative pursuits that might otherwise be pushed aside in a traditional marriage.

This section highlights the significance of passion projects and personal interests in the lives of those who remain unmarried. By focusing on what truly excites and inspires them, they create lives rich with joy, achievement, and creativity.

Unmarried individuals who embrace passion projects are often able to explore areas of interest without needing to balance the demands of a partner or family.

Take, for example, Sandra, an environmentalist who is deeply committed to wildlife conservation. She spends months in remote locations, volunteering with organizations that protect endangered species.

For Sandra, the choice not to marry meant she could follow this passion wholeheartedly, knowing it would be difficult to maintain such an unconventional lifestyle with the obligations that marriage might entail. Her life is filled with adventure, beauty, and a sense of mission that brings her immense satisfaction.

This section also touches on the freedom of singlehood in facilitating lifelong learning and personal growth. Without the constraints of traditional responsibilities, many single people engage in continuous self-development through reading, travel, or skill-building activities. Some take up artistic pursuits, like painting or music, while others may immerse themselves in sports, social causes, or spirituality.

Through these activities, they craft a life that feels balanced, enriched, and deeply fulfilling. For instance, Simon is a novelist who decided to devote his time to his writing after ending a long-term relationship in his thirties. Singlehood has allowed him to write full-time, focusing on his passion for storytelling without distractions.

Simon reflects that, without the freedom to dive deep into his creative work, he might never have reached the level of fulfillment he experiences today. Writing became more than a hobby or career; it became a purpose, a way to explore the human condition, and a way to reach out to others through his stories.

Simon's journey emphasizes that purpose is not exclusive to married life; it can flourish wherever a person devotes themselves fully to something meaningful.

For those who are single, passion projects often become integral to their identity and happiness. The freedom to cultivate interests without compromise is a unique advantage, enabling them to experience life on their own terms.

They demonstrate that meaningful lives are not just about achievements but about the journey of exploring what resonates deeply within oneself.

Summary:

In Crafting a Purposeful Life, we see that those who choose not to marry are not simply opting out of traditional roles; they are consciously constructing lives filled with purpose, joy, and meaning. This chapter invites readers to consider that life's purpose is not limited to relationships or family obligations but can be found in many areas, including work, passion projects, community, and personal growth.

People like Maria, Joshua, Sandra, and Simon remind us that purpose is an individual journey. They inspire us to look within, to ask what truly matters, and to pursue those passions wholeheartedly, regardless of relationship status. Through their stories, we learn that purpose and fulfillment are deeply personal choices that arise from commitment, passion, and a willingness to live authentically.

This chapter provides a powerful message: that a single life can be every bit as rich, meaningful, and impactful as any other. For those who may feel pressured to conform to societal norms, these stories offer reassurance and encouragement to embrace the unique path that feels right for them.

Chapter 3:

Navigating Relationships Outside of Marriage

While marriage is traditionally seen as the central relationship in a person's life, those who remain unmarried show us that love, connection, and companionship are not limited to a marital framework.

This chapter explores the depth, meaning, and fulfillment that can be found in relationships outside of marriage, from lifelong friendships to non-traditional romantic connections. It highlights the unique role that chosen relationships play in offering love, support, and joy, creating a community of connection and belonging for those who live independently.

The Power of Friendship

For unmarried individuals, friendships often become their primary source of emotional support, companionship, and love. Unlike marital relationships, which can come with legal and social expectations, friendships are chosen and maintained solely out of mutual affection and respect. This section delves into how friendships provide a powerful alternative to traditional partnerships, offering the love and support that might otherwise be expected in a marriage.

One of the great advantages of friendship is its flexibility. Many single individuals build "chosen families" with friends who fill roles that might otherwise be taken by a spouse. For instance, they may have a "best friend" who serves as their go-to confidant or a group of close friends who support one another through life's challenges.

These friendships are often intensely loyal, built on years of shared experiences, trust, and mutual understanding. For those who never marry, such friendships can be a source of comfort, joy, and stability throughout life.

Consider the story of Oliver and Jenna, two friends who have known each other since college. Both decided early on to remain single, finding fulfillment in their careers and personal lives. Over the years, they have shared countless experiences, celebrating each other's successes, traveling together, supporting one another through loss, and even moving to the same city to remain close. Their friendship is deeply fulfilling and mirrors the intimacy and loyalty often found in marriage.

For Oliver and Jenna, friendship isn't secondary to marriage; it's their chosen foundation for companionship and shared life experiences.

This section also examines how single individuals prioritize friendships in a way that differs from those in traditional partnerships. Without the time and energy commitments of a spouse or children, they often have more freedom to cultivate and invest deeply in these relationships.

This dedication to friendship allows them to experience a unique closeness with others, leading to bonds that are resilient and lasting. For those who choose to remain unmarried, friendship offers a unique kind of intimacy that brings fulfillment and depth to their lives.

The Role of Love Without Matrimony

Love without marriage is another dimension of single life that many embrace. Some people who remain single engage in romantic relationships that, while not leading to marriage, provide companionship, passion, and growth.

This section explores how non-traditional romantic relationships, whether brief or lasting, can be meaningful and fulfilling even without the structure of marriage.

In the lives of many unmarried individuals, romantic relationships serve as a form of companionship that allows them to experience love and intimacy without the formal commitments of marriage.

This can take various forms, from long-term partners who live separately to brief but impactful romantic connections. For instance, Christine, a woman in her fifties, has chosen to remain single after several serious relationships in her younger years.

She explains that each relationship offered valuable lessons, companionship, and love, but she ultimately felt that marriage would limit her independence. Now, she occasionally dates and experiences love and companionship on her own terms, finding a balance that works for her. Through her story, we see that love doesn't require a lifelong commitment to be meaningful.

This section also discusses the freedom that comes with experiencing love outside the constraints of marriage. Many single individuals find that, by not marrying, they have the flexibility to explore different kinds of connections without the pressure to settle or conform to societal expectations.

 Love, in this sense, is something they experience in ways that suit them at different stages of life, whether that's through brief, passionate encounters or deep, long-term companionship.

Some may also choose to cultivate "life partnerships" that aren't legally or socially recognized as marriages but carry similar commitment levels.

These partnerships allow for the emotional intimacy and support often associated with marriage, but with more flexibility and individual autonomy. These arrangements challenge the idea that marriage is the only way to experience lasting companionship, showing that love can be both deeply committed and adaptable to individual needs.

This section further explores how those who choose not to marry develop self-love as a foundational relationship. Many single individuals learn to be their own source of support and comfort, building resilience and self-worth that provide a strong foundation for navigating life's challenges.

Through self-care, self-reflection, and a commitment to personal growth, they create a loving relationship with themselves that fuels their independence and confidence. In this way, self-love becomes the anchor for all other relationships, allowing them to approach connections with others from a place of completeness.

For those who remain single, the role of love without matrimony is not about avoiding commitment or intimacy; it's about redefining love on their own terms. They embrace love as a fluid, evolving experience that enriches their lives in diverse ways, free from the expectations that often accompany marriage.

Summary:

In Navigating Relationships Outside of Marriage, we see that companionship and intimacy are not limited to marital bonds. Through powerful friendships, meaningful romantic relationships, and self-love, those who remain unmarried build rich networks of support and affection. They remind us that love, connection, and fulfillment come in many forms and that relationships outside of marriage can offer every bit as much depth, joy, and loyalty.

Through stories of individuals who find fulfillment in friendships and romantic connections outside the traditional marriage model, this chapter highlights the diverse ways we can experience meaningful relationships. For those who may question whether single life can be as rewarding as marriage, these narratives provide a powerful answer: that a life filled with love, belonging, and intimacy is not only possible but also flourishing outside of conventional norms.

This chapter encourages readers to redefine what it means to be "connected" and to see that love, whether found in friendship, romance, or self-acceptance, can be as fulfilling and impactful as any marriage. For those who choose this path, it's not about a lack of companionship; it's about creating a life where love and connection are defined by individual values and needs, leading to a truly authentic and deeply satisfying experience of relationships.

Chapter 4:

The Art of Living Solo

Living alone is often seen as a daunting prospect in a world that celebrates partnerships and family life, but for those who have chosen a single path, it can become a fulfilling art form.

This chapter explores how individuals who remain unmarried master the nuances of solo living, transforming solitude into a source of strength, creativity, and personal growth. The art of living solo is not merely about coping with being alone; it's about crafting a life that feels complete, satisfying, and rich in every aspect.

Embracing Solitude as a Source of Strength

For those who remain unmarried, embracing solitude is often one of the first steps toward self-discovery and personal empowerment. This section delves into how learning to be comfortable with one's own company is both a skill and a powerful tool for emotional resilience.

Many single people find that solitude offers a unique opportunity for self-reflection, growth, and creativity that can be challenging to achieve within the dynamics of partnership.

Living alone allows individuals to develop a deep sense of self-awareness. Without the constant presence of a partner, they are free to explore who they are, what they value, and what truly brings them joy. For instance, consider Ellie, a writer who found that solitude was a fertile ground for creativity.

Early in her twenties, Ellie decided to live alone, investing time in her passions, developing her writing skills, and learning to enjoy her own company. She discovered that by living alone, she had the mental and emotional space to create in ways that might have been challenging with a partner's presence.

Ellie's experience reveals how solitude can be an empowering choice, one that allows individuals to develop themselves deeply and create a life that feels whole on their own.

The process of embracing solitude also fosters self-reliance and resilience. Those who live solo learn to navigate life independently, managing both practical and emotional challenges on their own. Without a partner to rely on for daily support, they become adept at problem-solving, from handling finances to managing a household. This independence can lead to an inner strength and adaptability that serve them well throughout life, making them more resilient in the face of setbacks.

For many, this self-sufficiency is a point of pride, representing a life lived on their own terms.

Additionally, embracing solitude allows individuals to develop strong internal resources for handling loneliness. By learning to find comfort in their own company, they develop a deep sense of inner peace.

For those who remain single, solitude is not about feeling isolated or lacking companionship; it's about cultivating a relationship with oneself. This self-relationship becomes a source of strength, allowing them to move through life with confidence and a deep sense of security that is not dependent on anyone else.

Designing a Home and Life for One

The physical and emotional space of solo living also allows individuals to craft an environment uniquely suited to their tastes and lifestyle. This section explores how single people design homes that reflect their individuality, creating a sanctuary that is both a reflection of their identity and a source of comfort and joy.

Living alone means having the freedom to make one's own choices about how to decorate, organize, and inhabit a space, which can be deeply fulfilling.

Living solo gives individuals the freedom to design their living space without compromise. Whether they prefer minimalist decor or an eclectic array of personal mementos, they are free to build an environment that feels truly like home. For example, Marcus, a painter, shares how he transformed his small studio apartment into an artist's haven, filling it with inspiration, supplies, and art in progress.

His home reflects his creative energy and serves as a constant source of inspiration and motivation. Without the need to accommodate another person's tastes or needs, Marcus has crafted a space that feels fully his own and that brings him joy and fulfillment every day.

This section also examines the ways in which single people set routines and personal rituals that make living solo a fulfilling lifestyle. Without the demands of a partner or family, they can structure their day according to their own rhythms and preferences, developing habits that enhance their well-being.

For example, some might start their mornings with quiet meditation or end their evenings with a favorite book. Others, like Claire, a chef, take pride in cooking elaborate meals just for themselves, seeing this as an act of self-care and an expression of their culinary passion.

These routines help turn solo living into an art form, where every aspect of daily life is designed with intention and joy.

The freedom of solo living also allows for a greater focus on personal health and wellness. Many who live alone make conscious choices about how they spend their time and energy, often dedicating themselves to physical, mental, and spiritual self-care practices.

For those who enjoy exercise, a solo lifestyle allows for an uninterrupted commitment to physical wellness routines. Others focus on mental health, developing strong self-care practices, and prioritizing activities that bring peace and relaxation.

By living independently, they create lives that are not only tailored to their preferences but also deeply supportive of their health and happiness.

Lastly, solo living allows for flexibility and adaptability that can enhance personal growth. Without the need to consider another person's schedule or preferences, those who live alone can make decisions quickly and adapt to changes without negotiation. This freedom often leads to a sense of empowerment and fulfillment, as they are able to explore new hobbies, try out different career paths, or even relocate on a whim.

The flexibility inherent in solo living fosters a dynamic lifestyle where growth and change are embraced and supported by one's environment.

The Art of Living Solo

Summary:

In The Art of Living Solo, we see that solo living is not just a necessity but a conscious choice that many find fulfilling, empowering, and joyful. Those who live alone cultivate strength, resilience, and creativity through solitude, while designing lives and homes that reflect their individuality. For them, living solo is not about isolation but about the freedom to explore, grow, and live fully on their own terms.

The chapter illustrates how, for many, solo living is an art form that requires intention, creativity, and a strong relationship with oneself. It shows readers that a fulfilling life doesn't require a partner; it requires an understanding of one's own needs, desires, and passions. By fully embracing the advantages of solo living, these individuals demonstrate that happiness and purpose are achievable within a life designed for one.

The art of living solo is ultimately about autonomy, balance, and a commitment to personal well-being. Through the stories shared here, we see that living alone can lead to a life filled with joy, meaning, and fulfillment. For those who may fear solitude, this chapter serves as an invitation to rethink the possibilities of solo living, to see it as an empowering choice rather than a compromise, and to embrace the beauty of a life crafted independently.

Chapter 5:

Legacy and Impact on One's Own Terms

While legacy is often associated with family and the idea of passing something down to the next generation, those who choose a life outside of marriage redefine this concept in profound personal ways.

For individuals who remain unmarried, legacy and impact are not bound by traditional ideas of family lineage or material inheritance. Instead, their legacies are often shaped by the people they touch, the causes they champion, and the mark they leave through creative, intellectual, and humanitarian contributions.

This chapter explores the diverse ways that single individuals cultivate a lasting legacy, showing that a life lived independently can have a deep, meaningful, and far-reaching impact.

Redefining Legacy Beyond Family Lines

One of the most powerful aspects of legacy for single individuals is that they can define it entirely on their own terms. This section delves into how individuals who never married contribute to the world in ways that reflect their unique values, priorities, and passions.

Without the traditional family structure, they often turn to other forms of impact that allow them to leave something meaningful behind, whether it's in their professional work, creative projects, or community service.

Take, for example, Daniel, an environmental activist who dedicated his life to conservation efforts across the globe. Having chosen not to marry, Daniel's legacy isn't carried by children or family members; instead, it lives on through the policies he helped shape, the wildlife he helped protect, and the generations of young activists he inspired.

For him, legacy is measured not in family lineage but in the environmental progress he fostered. By focusing on conservation, he leaves a legacy that will benefit countless people and ecosystems long after he's gone. His work reflects a commitment to something greater than himself, creating a lasting impact through dedication to a cause he believed in deeply.

Similarly, the legacy for many singles is about mentorship and knowledge-sharing. Without traditional family responsibilities, many unmarried individuals devote time to mentoring young people or supporting others within their fields. By sharing their expertise, they leave a lasting impact on the lives and careers of others, shaping the future in a meaningful way.

For instance, Sophia, a renowned architect, spent decades mentoring aspiring architects, particularly women entering the field. She considers her legacy to be the thriving careers and innovative designs of those she mentored, who carry forward her insights, vision, and commitment to excellence.

Her story shows that legacy doesn't require direct lineage; it's about the lives one has touched, the skills one has passed down, and the inspiration one leaves behind.

For singles, the freedom from familial expectations allows them to focus on causes or communities that resonate most with their values. Legacy, in this sense, becomes about contributing to something enduring, whether that's through advocacy, volunteerism, or educational pursuits.

Many see this approach as equally significant to family legacy, as it allows them to make a difference that aligns closely with their personal beliefs and passions.

Creating a Life of Meaning and Influence

For unmarried individuals, legacy is closely tied to how they live each day, crafting a life that reflects their values and aspirations. This section explores how these individuals impact the world through their choices, values, and personal influence, leaving a lasting impression on those around them.

By pursuing a life of meaning, they create a ripple effect that reaches far beyond their immediate circles.

Living a life of meaning often means striving to make each moment purposeful and aligned with one's beliefs. For many single people, this translates to investing in projects, passions, or communities that bring personal fulfillment and leave a positive impact.

Consider the story of Malik, a writer and social justice advocate who dedicates his time to raising awareness about issues affecting marginalized communities. Malik has written several books and countless articles, using his words to educate and inspire. Through his work, he reaches people around the world, many of whom he may never meet, but who are influenced by his message.

His impact lies in the way he's changed perceptions, ignited conversations, and inspired action, a legacy of influence that is powerful and far-reaching.

For others, living a life of influence means embodying values that inspire those around them. In their communities and social circles, they become role models, showing that a life outside of marriage can be deeply fulfilling and impactful.

Alice, for example, has spent her life supporting local art programs in her town, organizing workshops, and creating public art facilities that beautify the community. Her influence has enriched the cultural landscape of her city, making art accessible to people of all ages. Alice's dedication to her community shows that a legacy can be built through ongoing contributions that uplift and enrich the lives of others.

Living solo often enables individuals to dedicate themselves wholeheartedly to their purpose. Without traditional family obligations, they have the freedom to pour energy and resources into projects that resonate with them deeply.

This independence can lead to impressive accomplishments, as they're able to prioritize their goals without compromise. For these individuals, their life's work becomes their legacy, a reflection of their passions, skills, and commitment. Through the impact of their work, they leave a mark that extends beyond their lifetime.

Finally, for some singles, legacy is found in small, daily acts of kindness and connection. While these contributions may not make headlines, they often leave a profound and lasting impression on those they touch. From offering support to friends and family to volunteering locally, they create a legacy of generosity, compassion, and empathy.

By living a life of integrity and kindness, they show that impact doesn't always require grand gestures; it can be built through consistent, meaningful interactions that uplift and inspire others.

Summary:

In Legacy and Impact on One's Own Terms, we see that legacy is a deeply personal journey, one that is shaped by our choices, values, and actions. For those who remain unmarried, legacy is not defined by family or tradition; it's about leaving a mark in ways that resonate with their beliefs, talents, and aspirations.

Their stories remind us that we all have the power to shape our impact, regardless of our relationship status.

This chapter challenges readers to rethink what it means to leave a legacy, showing that fulfillment and influence can come from lives lived independently. Through dedication to meaningful causes, mentorship, creativity, and kindness, single individuals create legacies that reflect their unique journeys.

They show us that legacy is not about who we leave behind, but about how we live and what we give to the world.

By embracing a legacy on their own terms, these individuals redefine what it means to make an impact. Their lives are a testament to the power of living authentically, and they encourage us all to think about how we can leave the world a better place, not just through traditional family roles, but through passion, commitment, and a desire to make a difference.

For those who have chosen a path outside of marriage, their legacy is proof that purpose, fulfillment, and impact are achievable through dedication to the causes, people, and ideas that matter most to them.

Chapter 6:

The Pressure to Marry

From childhood fairy tales to cultural traditions and subtle family remarks at gatherings, the idea that marriage is the ultimate achievement in adult life is everywhere. For many, it feels less like an option and more like a requirement.

Chapter 6 explores the persistent pressure to marry, where it comes from, how it shapes our decisions, and what it takes to walk a different path without apology.

Whether it's a well-meaning aunt asking, "So when is it your turn?" or a deeply ingrained belief that one's worth is tied to marital status, the societal push toward matrimony is real, and often relentless.

 Yet, an increasing number of individuals are choosing fulfillment outside of marriage and thriving. This chapter gives voice to those experiences, while offering guidance for how to navigate the complex landscape of societal expectations.

Cultural Expectations and Family Voices

Marriage is often woven into the fabric of cultural identity. In many communities, it's more than a romantic union; it's a rite of passage, a symbol of maturity, and a source of social status. When someone deviates from this path, it can be met with confusion, pity, or even disapproval.

Cultural expectations vary across ethnic, religious, and geographic lines. For example, in many traditional households, regardless of race, young women may be taught that their highest calling is to become a wife and mother.

Delaying or rejecting marriage can be viewed as defiance or failure. Even highly accomplished individuals may find their achievements minimized if they are not accompanied by a wedding ring.

Family voices add another layer of pressure. These voices are often loud during holidays, weddings, or milestone birthdays. Comments like "You're not getting any younger," or "You'll be lonely when you're older," come from a place of concern, but can be deeply hurtful. The assumption is clear: a single life is an incomplete one.

But choosing not to marry is not the same as choosing to be alone. Many who remain unmarried are surrounded by rich communities, deep friendships, and fulfilling careers.

They are caretakers, leaders, creatives, and visionaries. Redefining success means acknowledging that personal growth, service, and joy do not depend on marital status.

To push back against this pressure, it helps to:

Reaffirm your values and personal goals

Set boundaries with well-meaning family members

Educate others (gently) about different paths to fulfillment

When you live according to your truth, you give others permission to do the same.

The Silent Judgment of Society

The judgment of being unmarried can often be silent but powerful. It lurks in job interviews where employers subtly prefer "stable" married candidates, in medical forms that assume a spouse is an emergency contact, or in tax systems that offer better benefits to the married.

Women, in particular, face intense scrutiny. Unmarried women are sometimes labeled as "difficult," "unlucky," or even "selfish." Men might be questioned about their sexual orientation or assumed to be perpetual bachelors who "just haven't grown up."

These assumptions are damaging, not only because they're often untrue, but because they reduce individuals to a single, outdated narrative.

Social media amplifies the pressure. Engagement photos, wedding videos, and anniversary celebrations create a curated image that equates love with marriage and happiness with coupledom.

 For those who choose not to marry, the algorithm rarely reflects their joy. But a quiet revolution is happening. More people are sharing their stories about traveling solo, building businesses, raising children on their own, or simply living a full life without a partner.

Their courage helps challenge the default settings of society.

To combat silent judgment:

Find community with others who share your lifestyle

Celebrate your milestones, even if they don't involve rings

Speak openly about your choices when you feel safe to do so

Changing the narrative requires visibility.

Your story matters, and it has the power to shift societal norms for the better.

Breaking Free from the Timeline Trap

The "timeline trap" is the invisible script many people feel pressured to follow: graduate, get a job, marry by 30, have children by 35, and live happily ever after. When someone's life doesn't follow this script, it can feel like they've failed, when in fact, they may just be living authentically.

Breaking free from the timeline trap means questioning who wrote the script in the first place. Was it family? Religion? Movies? Society at large? And more importantly, does it reflect your true desires?

Many people discover, often later in life, that their deepest fulfillment comes not from ticking off milestones, but from following their intuition. Whether it's launching a business at 45, adopting a child at 50, or starting a new passion project at 60, life can unfold beautifully outside the traditional timeline.

Here are ways to reclaim your personal timeline:

Reflect on what success looks like to you, not what you've been told

Journal your dreams, goals, and purpose-driven ideas

Surround yourself with people who affirm your path

When you stop racing the clock, you start hearing your soul. You realize that living a meaningful life isn't about doing things on time, it's about doing the right things for you.

This chapter is a reminder that the pressure to marry, while real, doesn't have to define or derail you. You can honor tradition without being bound by it. You can listen to family without living for them. And most importantly, you can walk your own path, unwed, unshaken, and wholly fulfilled.

Summary:

The Freedom of Unapologetic Choices

This chapter celebrates the autonomy of unmarried individuals who make life choices based on personal values rather than societal expectations.

It explores the confidence that comes with choosing one's own timeline, how to handle judgment from others, and the liberation found in walking a path true to oneself.

Readers are encouraged to trust their instincts, embrace self-validation, and take pride in a life defined by authenticity, not conformity.

Chapter 7:

Financial Freedom and Independence

One of the most overlooked benefits of remaining unmarried is the financial autonomy it can provide. Without the need to merge incomes, compromise on spending habits, or manage joint financial decisions, individuals have the opportunity to define wealth on their own terms.

This chapter examines how those who remain single navigate money, build wealth, and use financial independence as a foundation for a life lived freely and deliberately.

Unmarried individuals often learn to become excellent stewards of their resources. Their financial journeys can be empowering stories of resilience, smart planning, and bold investments in themselves and their futures.

Budgeting, Saving, and Building Wealth Alone

When you're solely responsible for your financial well-being, budgeting becomes both a necessity and a tool of empowerment. While couples may have the benefit of dual incomes, they also share debt, responsibility, and compromise. Single individuals must learn to make every dollar work toward their vision.

Many unmarried adults craft thoughtful budgets that reflect their personal values. Whether it's saving for a dream trip, buying a home, or investing in their education, they learn early how to prioritize what matters.

Strategies include:

Living below your means

Automating savings and investments

Paying off debt quickly and strategically

These disciplined financial habits often result in a higher level of financial literacy and stronger personal credit, assets that provide stability and confidence.

Investing in Passions and Personal Growth

One of the most powerful aspects of financial freedom is the ability to invest in yourself. For those who never marry, this can mean exploring passions, starting businesses, or pursuing advanced degrees without needing approval or compromise.

Personal growth becomes a priority, not a luxury. Many use their resources to travel, learn new skills, or give back to their communities. Financial independence allows for a lifestyle that reflects their inner compass, not societal scripts.

Some real-life examples include:

Opening a yoga studio

Studying abroad in midlife

Donating to causes that matter deeply

Each choice becomes a reflection of who they are, and proof that wealth isn't just about money, but about how it empowers a purpose-driven life.

Preparing for the Future Without a Spouse

A critical element of financial independence for single adults is future planning. Without a spouse to rely on for care or income in later years, single individuals must take proactive steps to protect themselves.

This often includes:

Creating a solid retirement plan

Writing a will and assigning a power of attorney

Exploring long-term care insurance and health directives

Planning ahead ensures peace of mind and control over one's destiny. It also enables singles to age with dignity, on their own terms.

This chapter emphasizes that a solo financial path is not a burden; it is a roadmap to empowerment. When managed wisely, financial independence is the ultimate act of self-love and freedom.

Summary:

Spiritual Fulfillment and Inner Peace

Focusing on the spiritual dimensions of solo living, Chapter 7 highlights how many unmarried individuals find deep meaning through faith, meditation, nature, and creative expression.

It emphasizes the importance of nurturing the inner self, establishing a strong spiritual foundation, and cultivating peace that isn't dependent on a partner.

The chapter also examines how resilience, gratitude, and mindful living foster emotional stability and joy.

Chapter 8:

Embracing Spiritual and Emotional Fulfillment

For those who never married, fulfillment is not a void to be filled but a state of being, cultivated through meaningful experiences, inner peace, and spiritual connection.

Chapter 8 explores how emotional and spiritual satisfaction are integral to living a rich, wholehearted life.

This chapter dives into the diverse ways people connect with something greater than themselves, whether through faith, nature, community, or creativity, and how these paths contribute to a well-rounded, joyful life.

Finding Peace Within

A fulfilling life often begins with inner peace. For unmarried individuals, especially those who've chosen or accepted this path, self-reflection becomes a powerful tool.

The solitude of living solo provides ample space for developing a deeper relationship with oneself. This introspection helps cultivate emotional intelligence, leading to better emotional regulation, empathy, and resilience.

This section explores the practices that help maintain emotional health and peace: meditation, journaling, mindfulness, and prayer. We'll share stories of individuals who've turned inward to discover strength, purpose, and clarity, demonstrating how emotional fulfillment does not rely on external validation.

Case studies in this section highlight people who transformed loneliness into solitude and used their alone time to deepen their personal growth. Whether through therapy, artistic expression, or spending time in nature, they redefined what it means to be "whole" without a partner.

Exploring Spiritual Identity

Spirituality is often a cornerstone of a fulfilled life. This section addresses the role of faith and spiritual belief systems in shaping one's life outside the bounds of traditional marital structures.

Whether grounded in religion or personal belief systems, spiritual fulfillment provides a sense of purpose, belonging, and peace.

Some never-married individuals describe a divine calling that led them away from conventional relationships and into lives of service, creativity, or spiritual devotion.

Their sense of spiritual alignment often replaces the societal expectation to marry and have children.

We explore different spiritual paths, including Christianity, Buddhism, Indigenous practices, and secular humanism, that guide individuals toward inner peace.

Through interviews and reflections, readers will witness how spiritual identity can be a strong foundation for those who feel called to live beyond traditional roles.

Creating Joy Through Purposeful Living

This section ties emotional and spiritual fulfillment to purposeful living. Without the traditional milestones of marriage and family, unmarried individuals often seek purpose through their passions, community involvement, and creative endeavors.

We examine how people find joy through service, advocacy, travel, teaching, mentoring, and more. These purpose-driven activities foster a sense of connection and belonging that rivals, if not exceeds, that of traditional family life.

The stories shared here include entrepreneurs, artists, caregivers, and volunteers who infuse their lives with intentional joy.

Living with intention, focusing on what truly brings satisfaction, and giving back are all signs of an emotionally and spiritually fulfilled life.

This section encourages readers to reflect on their own purpose and invites them to embrace a holistic view of joy that isn't dependent on relationship status.

Summary:

Emotional Wellness and Self-Care

Chapter 8 tackles the often-overlooked need for emotional hygiene and intentional self-care in single living.

It discusses healthy boundaries, emotional independence, and practices for managing loneliness and stress. Self-nurturing routines and emotional awareness are framed not as luxuries but as necessities for thriving.

The chapter encourages a lifestyle rooted in self-respect, balance, and personal renewal.

Chapter 9:

The Financial Freedom of a Solo Life

While marriage often involves joint financial responsibilities and shared goals, single individuals navigate their economic paths independently. This chapter explores the financial freedom and challenges of a solo life, offering a nuanced look at how unmarried individuals plan, build, and secure their futures on their own terms.

With no spouse or children to support, many singles develop financial strategies that prioritize personal goals, long-term security, and meaningful investments.

Building Wealth on Your Own Terms

Financial independence is often a hallmark of unmarried life. Without the joint expenses and compromises that come with marriage, single individuals are free to create their own financial goals and pursue them without negotiation.

This section delves into the discipline, planning, and mindset required to build wealth alone. We explore the power of budgeting, investing, and living within one's means.

Real-life stories feature individuals who have purchased homes, invested in retirement accounts, or launched businesses without a partner.

These narratives dispel the myth that financial success requires a dual income or a traditional household structure.

Additionally, we explore the emotional aspect of money management, overcoming scarcity mindsets, building confidence in solo decision-making, and developing a healthy relationship with money that supports personal fulfillment and long-term peace.

Redefining Security and Stability

Traditional narratives suggest that marriage provides a stable and secure life. However, many singles have crafted their own versions of security, whether that means downsizing, moving abroad, or maintaining a flexible lifestyle that fits their values.

This section looks at how individuals redefine what security means for them. We discuss the importance of emergency funds, health insurance, wills, and long-term care planning. We also highlight how financial literacy and proactive decision-making allow unmarried individuals to feel empowered rather than vulnerable.

This section includes tools and tips for creating personalized safety nets and showcases stories of people who have used their financial flexibility to make unconventional but deeply rewarding life choices.

Spending for Fulfillment, Not Obligation

One of the most freeing aspects of unmarried life is spending money in ways that bring joy and purpose, free from societal or familial pressure.

This section celebrates the intentionality of choosing how to allocate resources in ways that enhance one's life.

We highlight those who spend money on travel, education, self-care, charitable giving, and passions that bring meaning and growth.

These stories challenge the idea that fulfillment comes from shared expenses or traditional milestones like weddings and children's education.

Ultimately, this section underscores that financial freedom is not just about wealth accumulation but about living fully and responsibly. It's about valuing experiences, making smart choices, and creating a financial life that supports your values.

Summary:

The Financial Freedom of a Solo Life

Living solo can provide unmatched financial clarity and freedom. Chapter 9 explores budgeting, investing, and financial planning without compromise.

Readers learn how to redefine security, build wealth independently, and spend with purpose.

This chapter reframes financial success as a personal endeavor and illustrates how unmarried individuals build legacies and achieve abundance on their own terms.

Chapter 10:

Celebrating Milestones Without a Marriage License

Traditional milestones, engagements, weddings, and anniversaries often take center stage in our cultural celebration of adulthood. But for those who never marry, life's most meaningful moments often go unrecognized by society.

Chapter 10 is a tribute to the accomplishments, growth, and personal achievements of the unmarried. It affirms that milestones are not confined to romantic relationships and that every individual deserves to celebrate the journey they've created for themselves.

Redefining Achievement and Celebration

For those living outside traditional norms, recognizing one's progress and growth becomes a deeply personal endeavor. This section explores how unmarried individuals redefine success and celebrate it in ways that feel authentic.

From promotions and relocations to birthdays and personal breakthroughs, unmarried individuals often mark significant moments with intention and joy.

The chapter explores how throwing a solo travel party, hosting a home blessing ceremony, or commemorating five years of therapy can be just as meaningful as any wedding celebration.

We also discuss the mental shift required to validate personal achievements without waiting for societal acknowledgment. Instead of feeling left out, these individuals carve out space to honor themselves, creating traditions that resonate with their lifestyle and beliefs.

Creating Rituals and Traditions That Matter

Rituals bring rhythm and meaning to life. While traditional rituals may revolve around marriage or family holidays, single people have the freedom to craft their own meaningful traditions.

Whether it's an annual solo vacation, a vision board brunch, or a personal day of reflection, these new rituals reinforce self-worth and joy.

This section showcases creative ways people celebrate themselves and their communities. We highlight individuals who host self-love retreats, celebrate the adoption of a pet, commemorate a book launch, or throw housewarming gatherings for their dream homes.

The goal is to empower readers to build traditions that honor their values, encourage reflection, and bring people together, whether they have chosen family, lifelong friends, or new communities.

By doing so, we honor the beauty in living life on one's own terms.

Embracing a Life of Continual Growth

Milestones don't stop at a certain age, and unmarried individuals are uniquely positioned to continue evolving without being bound by conventional timelines. This final section celebrates lifelong learning, transformation, and joy.

We share stories of individuals who went back to school at 50, started a business at 60, or began a spiritual journey in their 40s. Their paths remind us that personal development is a continual process and that every step forward is worthy of acknowledgment.

Embracing a growth mindset allows unmarried individuals to find joy in everyday victories, knowing that every chapter of their life is part of a rich, meaningful journey. It's a reminder that milestones, no matter how big or small, are valid and worth celebrating.

Summary:

Celebrating Milestones Without a Marriage License

This chapter shines a light on the countless meaningful moments unmarried people experience that deserve celebration.

From career advancements to spiritual milestones and personal growth, readers are reminded that fulfillment isn't limited to traditional life events.

The chapter encourages creating personal rituals, defining success on one's own terms, and embracing lifelong growth through every phase of life.

A Life Fully Lived, Freely Chosen

Why I Never Married? Unwed–Unshaken, Living Life on My Own Terms is not just a personal narrative; it's a movement. It is a reminder that choosing to remain unmarried is not an absence of love, commitment, or purpose; it's an affirmation of autonomy, joy, and intentional living.

This book challenges outdated ideas about what it means to be whole and instead offers an empowered blueprint for living fully and freely.

Each chapter has been a step toward dismantling myths, redefining success, and honoring the people who live beautifully outside society's expectations.

Whether you've never married, chose a different path, or are simply curious about what life could look like beyond the altar, this book proves that fulfillment, meaning, and legacy come in many forms.

To every reader who has questioned their path, may you walk forward with confidence. To those who feel unseen, may you find your reflection in these pages.

And to those quietly living their truth—unwed, unshaken—know that your life is not second-best. It is sovereign. It is sacred. And it is yours.

Acknowledgements

Writing this book has been a deeply personal journey, and it wouldn't have been possible without the support, inspiration, and insights of so many people.

To my family, thank you for supporting me as I explored what it means to live a full life on my own terms. Your encouragement allowed me to embrace the path I chose and to share these stories with honesty and joy.

To my friends, especially those who have shared their own experiences of living solo, thank you for your trust, wisdom, and encouragement. Your lives have inspired many pages of this book, and I'm grateful for the memories, conversations, and laughter that continue to enrich my life.

To everyone who shared their stories for this book, thank you for opening your hearts and allowing your unique journeys to serve as examples of courage and independence. Your voices will resonate with readers and remind them of the beauty of living authentically.

Why I Wrote This Book

I wrote this book because some stories deserve to be honored; not in whispers or passing conversations, but in bold, beautiful print that says: You matter. Your life matters. What you've given can never be repaid, but it will never be forgotten.

This book is dedicated to you, Lady Di.

For over 40 years, you have loved this family through the unimaginable. You gave up what many chase, a husband, children, a life centered around your own dreams, so you could care for the elders, the sick, and the wounded hearts no one else knew how to hold. You were the nurse, the counselor, the cook, the peacekeeper, and the glue. You never asked for applause. You simply showed up. Day after day. Year after year.

I've watched you patch broken spirits, bury your own dreams quietly, and carry burdens others never noticed. But I noticed. We noticed. And more than that, we love you for it.

This book was written to reflect the kind of strength you embody. To say out loud what too often goes unsaid: You are a living example of selflessness, resilience, and unwavering love. You have lived a life that didn't follow the script, and yet, you've created a masterpiece.

Through these pages, I hope you see yourself, not just as the caregiver or the backbone, but as the hero. The woman who made hard choices out of love. The one who stood in the fire and still managed to give warmth to others. The one who didn't marry, but who has loved more deeply and more sacrificially than most ever will.

This is not just a book. It's a love letter to you. From me. From us. From everyone whose life you've touched.

You are deeply seen. You are profoundly loved. And you will always, always be honored.

With all my heart,
Vgdawson

Helpful Resources:

Singlehood and Life Satisfaction

Research has increasingly shown that single people can experience life satisfaction comparable to or greater than that of married individuals. The decision not to marry can often be rooted in a desire for autonomy, personal fulfillment, and self-determination, all factors associated with life satisfaction.

The Psychological Benefits of Solitude and Independence

For individuals who choose not to marry, independence and solitude can offer psychological benefits such as self-reflection, self-reliance, and emotional well-being. Research supports the idea that time spent alone fosters personal growth and can lead to a greater sense of self-knowledge and purpose.

Meaningful Relationships Beyond Marriage

Single individuals often develop deep, meaningful relationships with friends, family, and community members. These relationships can provide emotional support and fulfillment, serving as a vital aspect of life satisfaction and resilience.

Redefining Legacy and Impact for Unmarried Individuals

Many single people redefine the concept of legacy, focusing on community impact, mentorship, and creative achievements rather than traditional family legacies. This shift demonstrates how unmarried individuals make unique contributions to society.

Challenging Societal Expectations and Stereotypes about Marriage

Societal expectations often promote marriage as a pathway to happiness, but research suggests that happiness and fulfillment can be equally achieved by those who remain single. This research encourages a broader understanding of life satisfaction that includes diverse life paths.

Leave a Review

If this book touched your heart, please let the world know.

Your review matters more than you know. It helps other readers, especially those struggling with silent pain, find a story that makes them feel seen, heard, and understood. Whether it's a few words or a heartfelt paragraph, your voice has power.

Please take a moment to leave a review on:

📚 Amazon

📚 Goodreads

📚 Barnes & Noble

Your words could be the reason someone chooses healing over holding on.

Thank you for sharing this journey with me.

With gratitude,
Vgdawson

Stay Connected with Me

This isn't goodbye. This is just the beginning.

If this book spoke to your soul, I invite you to join my inner circle, a place for women (and men) who are ready to grow, heal, and walk in truth together.

📩 Subscribe to the "Letters from vgdawson" Newsletter

Get exclusive reflections, behind-the-scenes writing updates, journal prompts, book releases, and self-care tools delivered straight to your inbox.

📬 Sign up at: www.what2buynext.com/newsletter

📲 Follow on Social Media:

Instagram | YouTube | TikTok: @what2buynext

Website: www.what2buynext.com

Together, let's keep writing new chapters.

Chapters of peace, purpose, and power.

You deserve every bit of it.

Warmly, *Vgdawson*

I Need to Think About My Life Choices

We don't always know when we're at a crossroads

Vgdawson

A Journal for Reflecting on Life Choices" is a transformative self-help journal designed to guide you through a thoughtful and introspective journey. This journal encourages you to reflect on your life choices, fostering a deeper understanding of your decisions and their impact on your life.

Through engaging prompts and insightful questions, "I Need to Think" helps you explore your inner thoughts, clarify your goals, and cultivate a more meaningful and purposeful life. Dive into this journal to challenge your thinking patterns, reshape your mindset, and embark on a path of self-discovery and personal growth. This is the first in a series of journals dedicated to helping you live your best life.

Author of books on relationships, personal growth, and life transitions.

Friends for Life

How to grow & keep
friendships for a lifetime

Vgdawson

Friendship is one of the most
powerful relationships we
experience in life—
yet it's often the one we
understand the least.
**In *Friends for Life: How to
Grow and Keep Friendships
for a Lifetime*,** you're invited
into an honest, soul-centered
conversation about what it
truly means to build

friendships that last. This is not a book about surface-level
connections or temporary companionship. It's about the friends who
walk with you through seasons of growth, change, joy, and
heartbreak—and the wisdom it takes to nurture those bonds with
intention.
Whether you're cherishing lifelong friends, navigating shifting
connections, or learning how to be a better friend yourself, *Friends for
Life* meets you where you are. It reminds you that meaningful
friendship doesn't happen by accident—it's built through presence,
honesty, and care.
This book is for anyone who believes that friendship is not just a part
of life, but one of its greatest gifts.

Author of books on relationships, personal growth, and life transitions.

The Truth About Aging

What Your 50s, 60s, and 70s Will Show

Vgdawson

The Truth About Aging offers a clear, faith-grounded examination of what time reveals — in your body, your finances, your relationships, your emotional patterns, and your walk with God.

This is not a fear-based book about getting older.

It is a steady Christian perspective on how decades of habits, decisions, and beliefs compound — and how God remains faithful through every season.

Aging is not sudden.

It is accumulated.

In your 50s, the shift begins.

In your 60s, the audit becomes clearer.

In your 70s, refinement is unavoidable.

But aging is not only physical or financial — it is spiritual.

Thank You

Thank you to my readers. Whether you have chosen a life outside of marriage or you are simply curious about this path, your interest in this book means the world to me. My hope is that these stories resonate with you, inspire you, and perhaps even challenge your own assumptions about what it means to live fully.

Thank you for being part of this journey, and may this book encourage you to live boldly, pursue your passions, and embrace the life that feels most true to you.

"LIVING LIFE ON MY OWN TERMS"

www.ingramcontent.com/pod-product-compliance
Lightning Source LLC
Chambersburg PA
CBHW051006050726
47592CB00007B/2732